From Darkness to Light

From Darkness to Light

Raj Kumar, Ph.D

1stBooks – rev. 2/6/01

About the Book

From Darkness to Light is a book that will teach you how to achieve real happiness, how to make a balance in life, how to attain self-realization and communicate with God, a higher point of view, directions to cleanse confusions, conflicts and emotional disturbances from subconscious mind and to comfort your spirit.

"In him was life, and the life was the light of Men. Jesus said, "I am the light of the world. He who follows me shall not walk in darkness, but have the light of life."

John 1:4,8:12

Important Note:

Never force your breathing system when attempting breathing techniques or following the methods of meditation as described in this book. Consult with your physician, spiritual master or qualified instructor before attempting any technique or method. The author/publisher disclaims any implied warranties or merchantability of liability, loss or injury in connection with any of the techniques, methods or instructions.

ACKNOWLEDGMENT

I would like to express my love and gratitude to the following people:

-- Margeret Dikel who helped me edit this book

-- Andrew Cha who designed the cover page of this book

-- Mark Dichner, Ph.D. and Florence Takazawa who encouraged me to complete this book

-- Clifford Okumoto, M.D. for being such a great example of self-referral

-- Satguru Sivaya Subramununiyaswami for being my Guru and guiding me to the path of light through his teachings

-- Late Minal Kumar whose ideals and dedication to serve others became a great example for me to do something meaningful for others

-- Mike Tamanaha, Ted Goldman, Lester Matsumoto, Paul Kanehiro, Dan Yamada and Aaron Arakaki for being good friend and role models to serve handicapped individuals at Waimano Training School & Hospital

-- President Bill Clinton and Governor Benjamin J. Cayetano to appreciate my thoughts for mankind

DEDICATION

This book is dedicated to my parents who were my first teachers; to my brother, Dr. Krishan Kumar, a nature lover, philosopher and guide; to my teacher, Dr. Yashvir Singh and his wife, Kamlesh, who helped me in completing my Ph.D. in Psychology during my stay in Agra (India); to my sister, Santosh, and her husband, Yash Nagpaul, who helped me to stay after my arrival to the United States; to my wife, Sunita, a good friend who is spiritual, loving, caring and a wonderful mother: to my daughter, Sapna, for being the inspiration, real treasure and living expression of love and joy.

It is also dedicated to Goddess Saraswati, the mother of love, wisdom, knowledge, purity, beauty, compassion, peace, truth, forgiveness, light, energy and freedom. In Sanskrit language, the main prayer/mantra for Goddess Saraswati is as follows: "Asto ma sat gamaya, tamso ma jyotir gamaya." It means, "O mother, take me away from the darkness (ignorance) to light (wisdom).

TABLE OF CONTENTS

GOD

God is the source of everything in this universe
He gives life, wisdom, strength, and love
He gives energy and healing through Sun, Moon, Earth, Food,
Air and Water
He is always a giver, expecting nothing in return except love

He is almighty and he can be felt everywhere
He is in atom, nature, ocean and even in a grain of sand
He is invisible but he can be seen through inner eyes
He is unheard but he can be heard through silence and
meditation

When we become the verse, he becomes the song
When we become the waves, he becomes the shore
When we become lover and beloved, he becomes love
When we become spiritual students, he becomes the Master

He loves those who love others and themselves
He blesses those who always pray and purify themselves
He protects those who create peace for others and themselves
He meets those who serve others and take care of themselves

The children are different but the father is one
The religions are different but the philosophy is one
The paths are different but the goal is one
The names and forms are different but God is one

Man is fashioned by his faith: As faith is, so he is
God is not in the pleasure of senses, wealth and objects
God is not in the past and not in the future
God is in each breath, heart, love and in the present.

RELIGIONS

There are many religions in this world. All teach that there is a God and we are a part of God. Most of this information come from holy books and priests or spiritual leaders. Everyone has a different way of presenting the same information but the essence of all teachings is to love each other. The way religion is practiced today, it creates barriers between man and man and sows the seeds of hatred instead of binding us to God. We forget and do not realize that we are the sons of the same father who has no religion, caste or creed, nor is he in any one place or limited to any one person, society or nation. He is in all of us. If we love anyone, we love God. If we hate anyone, we hate God. The most important thing in everyone's life is to know yourself-- who you are, what is your purpose of life, what are your family, social and worldly duties, how to share love and serve others unconditionally, how to live peacefully, how to progress spiritually, and ultimately how to achieve liberation and unite with God.

PHILOSOPHY AND THE PRINCIPLES OF SPIRITUAL LIVING

Your personality and philosophy of life is shaped by your parents, your education, your religious beliefs, your interests, your inner attitude, your habits, likes and dislikes, your company, your actions and your environment. Thoughts are the seeds of your actions. If you plant good thoughts in your mind, then the fruit (actions) will be good, but if you plant bad or negative thoughts in your mind, then the fruits (actions) will also be bad. One who always thinks positively knows the purpose of life, strives for knowledge, loves all creatures, has good intentions to help others, and lives peacefully. He/she knows the art of living and leads a good life. The philosophy and principles of spiritual living include the following:

1. God is supreme
2. The body is mortal and the soul is immortal
3. All human beings are equal
4. Never judge others by color, race, sex, gender, language or disability
5. Treat everyone with respect and dignity
6. Maintain higher, positive thinking
7. Maintain simplicity in life style
8. Be truthful
9. Practice non-injury
10. Practice non-stealing
11. Practice non-attachment
12. Maintain discipline in character
13. Choose the right occupation and be dedicated to your work
14. Maintain love and respect toward your family and dedicate yourself to serve the family
15. Respect all religions and masters
16. Keep the right attitude
17. Maintain honest dealings with others
18. Speak good words and do good deeds

19. Follow the spiritual path, praying and meditating daily
20. Maintain control over mind and senses
21. Eat vegetarian food
22. Fast
23. Keep a consciousness of higher self
24. Keep a consciousness of God
25. Pilgrimage

GOD, SUN, MOON AND HUMANS

GOD   G - Generator   O - Operator   D - Destructor

G - God has created this universe
O - God is operating this universe
D - God will destroy this world when there are too many sins on this earth

Space is the father where earth is the mother.
Man is the sun where woman is the moon.
We are a part of God, the universe and nature.

The universe and human beings cannot survive without the sun and the moon. The presence and combination of the Sun and moon creates and maintains the cosmic energies in this universe. The sun rules and controls the planet for two weeks and then the moon rules and controls the planet for another two weeks. Most of man's energy (about 70%) comes from the sun and the rest (about 30%) comes from the moon. On the other side, most of the woman's energy (about 70%) comes from the moon and the rest (about 30%) comes from the Sun. These warm and cold energies create strength and love in the human body. Sun energy moves through the right nostril to the right hemisphere of the brain, and the moon energy moves through the left nostril to the left hemisphere of the brain. The combination of warm and cold energy maintains the temperature in the mind and body. Whenever there are changes in the size and position of sun and moon or they go through an eclipse, the planet, energies, colors, light and human beings and other creatures are all affected in a positive or negative way. The best and happiest day on earth comes when moon reaches its full size, facing the sun directly and sending river of light and love on the earth. Each individual experiences these affects differently. If you do not have a balance in the flow of warm and cold energies, then your mood is disturbed frequently. When this happens, check both nostrils. If you find that your left nostril is blocked, then close the left nostril with the index finger, breathe in through the right nostril

7

and exhale through the left nostril and meditate on the Moon. If you determine that your right nostril is blocked, then use the same method to open the right nostril and then meditate on the Sun. This process will balance the energy, keep you happy and healthy, and allow you to connect yourself with sun, moon and God easily.

NATURE

Nature is the most beautiful creation of God. Everyone is born out of nature and goes back to nature when the breath ends and the soul departs from the body. Nature is full of colors, beauty and vibrant energy. Life becomes beautiful when you live in nature. Beauty is everywhere in nature but it depends how you look at it and how you feel it. Looking at nature awakens the inner happiness and creativity. Mother Nature nourishes life, cures diseases and heals body, mind and soul.

THE UNIVERSAL DRAMA

God is the creator of the whole universe. God is the super director of the movie of everyone's life. He wrote the story of life before any one came to this world. Life is a universal drama where earth is the big stage. Each individual has been given a role to play according to his/her performance (Karma) in his/her previous life. The greatest challenge is playing your role positively and successfully until the drama of life ends.

THE WORLD

The human world is a place of existence. It is a place of repeated cycles of birth and death. All human beings go through the stages of birth, childhood, and adulthood until they ultimately meet death. Every human being experiences happiness, sadness, sickness, suffering and changes in life. One who has God and death consciousness and leads a simple and spiritual life will remain free from attachment, anxieties, fears and depression.

MEANING OF LIFE

You are very fortunate to have a human life verses an animal. Animals cannot think, talk, meditate or nor make the best choices during the periods of their life. They simply enjoy eating, sleeping and mating. If you have these same goals of life, then there is no use being born as a human being. Do not be lazy and do not indulge yourself in bad habits. Wake up and realize that this body is mortal. Use your intelligence and consciousness to meditate, to communicate with God, and to do something meaningful for mankind.

Life is a wonderful gift of God, thank Him everyday
Life means consciousness, love and precious moments; feel and enjoy everyday
Life is a universal drama, play a positive role everyday
Life is full of changes, accept and adjust with the changes everyday
Life is an inspirational song, sing it everyday
Life is a challenge, face it bravely
Life is a puzzle, solve it creatively
Life is a sport, play it enthusiastically
Life is a unique painting, color it artistically
Life is a journey, flow with it patiently
Remember life is very short, so live happily

BREATH AND MIND

The universe is filled with vibrant cosmic energy. The air contains the same cosmic energy. Each incoming breath maintains the life force (Prana), which further regulates the energy through the lungs, diaphragm, spine, cells, arteries and heart. The heart pumps blood to the brain, veins, inner organs and other parts of the body. No one can be alive without breath. Breath is life. Breath is a bridge between body and mind and between soul and universe. Thoughts flow with the movement of our breath. When we learn to focus on our breath, we are able to slow down our breath. When we are able to slow down our breath, our mind relaxes, our concentration increases, we can remove layers of darkness and we become aware of our negative emotions. When we become aware of our negative emotions, our inner awareness increases and we recognize our higher self. When we become aware of our higher self, we are able to use our willpower. When we are able to use our willpower, we are able to control our reactions to the senses. When we are able to control our reactions to the senses, we are able to control our mind, and when we are able to control our mind, we no longer remain the slave of our mind. The spirit becomes free.

ENERGY

No one can talk or move without energy. Life energy comes from cosmic powers, air, water and food. When energy is spent too fast or wasted through excessive mental/physical work, excessive speech, excessive sex or by holding negative emotions, then brain chemistry changes and the flow of energy is blocked, which further affects one's ability to think clearly, concentrate. It affects our mood, behaviors, adjustment with our external environment, health and life span.

DESTINY

Each human being is a beautiful creation of God. Life starts with breath, hunger, thirst and sleep. Each child is born with fate and his/her fate increases or decreases according to his/her deeds in life.

You are the creation of God
You are the reflection of your parents
You are the product of your childhood

You are what you believe
You are what you think
You are what you speak

You are what your association is with others
You are how you act or behave
You are what choices you make

You receive what you give to others
You experience what your desires are
What your desires are, so are your deeds
And what your deeds are, so is your destiny.

THE MAGIC OF MIND AND SENSES

We think clearly when our mind has no conflicts, anxieties, anger nor material desires and our mind is totally relaxed.

- We see more clearly when our attention is focused on a single object.

- We hear more clearly when we practice staying silent.

- We feel real bliss when we touch someone with love or we are touched with love.

- We develop patience and heal our body when we choose the right food, feel the taste on our palate and eat slow.

- We breathe better and smell more clearly when our consciousness is higher and our being is still.

UNIVERSAL LANGUAGE

Love is the only language that does not need any words to express itself. The language of love is transmitted, received and felt in the heart.

26

SUPER CONSCIOUSNESS

The stage of super consciousness is achieved only through Meditation. One who meditates regularly and has good control over anger, lust, greed, Ego and attachment finds a center within the self, awakens inner powers, and becomes aware of his/her own existence, nature and environment. He/she can visualize impossible things and objects that are beyond the power of ordinary people. He/she can achieve major things without any major efforts. He/she can also transmit messages to a person who may be miles away and can predict major future happenings. Super consciousness includes the following:

1. Consciousness of breath movement
2. Consciousness of the higher self
3. Consciousness of God
4. Consciousness of thoughts, emotions and feelings
5. Consciousness of the body, its needs, tension, pain and pleasure
6. Consciousness of the present
7. Consciousness of weather/nature (light, air, sound, colors and temperature)
8. Consciousness of worldly duties and actions/deeds
9. Consciousness of the environment (smell, objects, their colors, shapes, sizes, depth, sound and movements)
10. Consciousness of others (people, birds and animals)
11. Consciousness of time, work, upcoming things, appointments, changes and events
12. Consciousness of cosmic powers and universe
13. Consciousness of aging and death

"Consciousness is life and God is the life of our life."

ACTION/KARMA (CAUSE & EFFECT)

The universe has a super data bank which is directly connected with our mind. All of our actions (good or bad) are being recorded daily. Universal law says that each action has a reaction. Whatever we have done in the past, either good or bad, we will experience the results in the present. What we will experience in the future, depends on the actions we take today.

"Whatever you sow, so shall you reap."

"What goes around, comes around."

SPEECH AND SILENCE (Active Mind and Silent Mind)

Speech is the expression of thoughts, ideas and emotions
Silence is the reception and understanding of thoughts, ideas and emotions

Speech needs someone to interact, share thoughts and feelings
Silence needs no one except the self and nature

Speech makes friends and foe
Silence only makes friends

Speech expends mental energy
Silence saves and restores mental energy

Speech is subjective
Silence is objective

Speech educates others
Silence helps educate oneself

Speech demands something
Silence shows respect

Speech hurts feelings
Silence unites hearts

Speech agitates the mind
Silence creates calmness in the mind

Speech clutters the mind
Silence cleans the mind

Speech has limitations
Silence is infinite

Speech creates noise
Silence creates peace

Speech makes sound and movement
Silence maintains stillness in the mind

Speech is human
Silence is union with God

HIGHEST SERVICE

We live in a world where everyone and everything is interconnected. Service is an essential and important part of our daily life. When we love ourselves and the people who are around us, our each thought and action creates beauty, a good energy flows in the environment, and we feel a deep satisfaction in our hearts and minds. Service done with good intention and without expectation of something in return brings good results. Do your work as worship and remember that the highest duty of life is to help and serve others.

HAPPINESS

Happiness is a basic and permanent state of mind. It manifests when the mind is relaxed. One who has control over the mind and senses, cannot be disturbed with any temptation of objects, attachment, problems and other external happenings. He/she finds real happiness within the self, not in material things.

If you want happiness for one minute - smile
If you want happiness for one hour - relax
If you want happiness for one day - meditate
If you want happpiness for one week - make love
If you want happiness for one month - take vacation
If you want happiness for one year - think positive and do good deeds
If you want happiness for whole life - control your desires and stay healthy

ATTITUDE

Attitude is the major part of our character and personality. Good and bad attitudes come from our thoughts, speech and actions. We make friends and enemies because of our attitude. Positive attitude makes positive changes but negative attitude affects harmony, relationship, unity and productivity.

Have purity in your mind and heart.
Whatever you think, think positively.
Whatever you speak, speak sweet words.
Whatever you do, do it with love.

PATIENCE

Patience is the greatest characteristic of an individual. One who is calm and is patient in learning things, speaking and doing things, does things well and maintains good relationships with others. One who is impatient, always rushes to do things, makes mistakes and causes accidents, and creates disharmony in the environment. Develop more patience by eating slowly, relaxing and meditating daily. Remember that patience is the key to all success in life.

SUCCESS

You should not struggle so much for wealth or material possessions. The more you struggle and run after material things, the more you lose mental concentration and peace of mind. Good opportunities come to you when you focus your attention and energy away from several goals/directions to only one goal/direction. Only then is success more likely. Perform your duties in life without expectation of good results. Good things happen when you are least worried about the outcome of your actions.

The keys to success are:

- Concentration
- Confidence in yourself
- Faith in God
- Courage
- Enthusiasm
- Strong thoughts
- Right attitude
- Patience
- Honesty
- Good vision
- Good planning
- Good actions
- Good communication
- Good luck
- Good service
- Hard work
- Teamwork
- Network

SATISFACTION

The world is full of attractions and distractions. There is no end to human desires. The mind always want to experience more new things which causes more suffering. Learn to control your mind and senses and stop running after things. The more you run after different things, the more you throw energy out into the world and you lose the connection with your higher self and God. You are never satisfied and things become harder to achieve. Thank God everyday for what you have whether it is little or more. Be satisfied and lead a simple and happy life.

PROSPERITY

Prosperity does not come from wealth and material possessions. Prosperity is an internal experience of the self and the richness of life. How do you use your awareness? How do you feel about yourself? What do you do for others? What do you receive from others? How do you grow spiritually? Prosperity increases and multiplies when you give love and knowledge to others, show gratitude and care, appreciate others' help and receive love, support and blessings from others.

SINCERITY

Sincerity is part of our nature. Sincerity comes when we recognize our real self, understand our inner nature, and do things honestly. When we become more sincere about our self and our worldly duties, then our maturity increases and we feel more satisfaction in life.

PERSONAL GROWTH

Personal growth does not mean an increase in wealth, possessions or family

Personal growth means knowing and understanding your inner nature

Personal growth means working on the complete development of the character and the self

Personal growth means having full awareness of your own thoughts, actions and the outcome of actions

Personal growth means moving from dependence to independence

Personal growth means improving your own weaknesses and bad habits

Personal growth means behaving maturely and making mature decisions

Personal growth means using wisdom and patience to handle problems

Personal growth means having increased interpersonal skills and friendship with others

Personal growth means taking initiatives and fulfilling worldly duties positively

Personal growth means removing false beliefs and using judgment and experience in all situations

Personal growth means having increased confidence and courtesy in dealing with others

Personal growth means moving energy from the (ego) lower level to the (spiritual) higher level

The ultimate meaning of personal growth is expanding knowledge, understanding the meaning of life and the function of the world.

LOVE AND MARRIAGE

Life is incomplete without marriage and a marriage is incomplete without love and children. Marriage means:

M - Mutual
A - Appreciation
R - Respect
R - Romance
I - Intimacy
A - Acceptance
G - Gentleness
E – Emotions

CREATIVITY

Creativity comes from creative thoughts and creative thoughts come when the mind is totally relaxed and you are harmonized by love and nature. The more you observe and feel the nature around you, the more your consciousness increases and you start to think deeply about God, the real self, the world, the function of nature and the purpose of life. Give time to yourself, love yourself, love others, love nature and express your creative thoughts through good speech, creative planning for goals, creative writing, creative painting, singing, dancing, creating good things and creating a beautiful environment for yourself and others.

HUMILITY

Humility is the opposite of ego. Humility comes from the heart. The more humble you become, the more you are appreciated and acknowledged by others, as all human beings want to be treated with love and respect. Learn from nature. For example, when the trees grow and develop branches, leaves, fruits, flowers, they bend down and give shade and fruits. Be the same way when you grow. As you become stronger or richer, be more humble. Then you will be connected with everyone.

CHARITY

Selfless giving to support God's work on earth is one of the major purpose of everyone's life. Charity means sharing love and wealth with poor and helping religious institutions, schools and hospitals in the communities. Most of the scriptures suggest that people should give ten percent of their income each month or at the end of the year to the choice of their institution. One should not donate wealth, objects and property for fame. When a charity is given with good intention to help others it brings deep satisfaction and good fortune.

BLISS

Bliss is cosmic and the highest state of happiness. The experience of bliss is beyond the emotions and senses. When your thoughts are pure and you have true love with your loved one and God, then you experience bliss. Bliss is being loving, being joyful and being peaceful.

FAITH

Those who have faith in God are very close to God, and they are the blessed and strongest people on earth. God helps, guides and protects them at all times and in all situations of life. Faith in God means having no fear.

FREEDOM

Freedom means having the power to think, speak, act and live freely. Freedom is guided and felt by the soul not by the mind and desires. Following the commands of the mind leads to attachment, anger, delusion and suffering, but following intuitive messages of the soul and using wisdom and knowledge leads to liberation.

PRAYERS

Prayers have vibrant power and work miracles. Prayers are the easiest thing to transmit in any part of the universe. Prayers which are done with a pure heart and love bring quick and positive help and changes, especially during sickness and crisis. Prayers work faster and better than anything. The simplest prayers are as follows:

Dear God/Lord, give me love and the wisdom to think positively and to make good decisions in daily life.

Dear God/Lord, give me strength and courage to face the challenges of life.

Dear God/Lord, bless me and protect me from all troubles and dangerous situations.

Dear God/Lord, give me more knowledge and healing power to help heal others.

Dear God/Lord, my family member/friend needs healing as she/he is suffering from disease/accident.

Dear God/Lord, please keep peace on earth.

PEACE

Peace can be achieved only when you love yourself and others and give enough time to yourself to restore your energy through silence. As you practice feeling the silence within you and around you and focusing on your third eye (between the eyebrows), your inner concentration increases and the waves of thoughts slow and become still and inner peace is felt. This peace will move from forehead to your heart and then to each cell of your body. Find a center within yourself and you will become a center among others. Wherever you go, you will create peace and peace will flow from families to societies and from societies to the whole world.

"You are a lake of peace which merge into a big ocean and God is the ocean of peace"

TRUE KNOWLEDGE

No one is born with knowledge. Knowledge comes from parents, teachers, education and personal experience in life. Most of us use only 10% of our intellectual powers and 90% of our intellectual powers are fainted in our unconscious mind as our conscious and subconscious minds are too full with the past memories and are preoccupied with thoughts, worries and unknown fears of future. True knowledge begins when you stop swinging between past and future, so empty your subconscious mind and fill it with positive thoughts. Detach yourself from worldly matters and search for a real master. The real master is a messenger of God and has the key to the treasure of knowledge locked in your Kundalini (located in the base of the spine). When the time is right and you are ready, the real master will appear. He/she will initiate, bless and guide you in opening the hidden treasure through meditation, chanting and devotion to God. When the Kundalini is awaken and rises up through the spine to the third eye, you will feel a bliss, you will be enlightened, you will gain true knowledge, you will feel heavenly experience, and you will be connected to and united with God and will start to say, "I am in heaven, I am with God, God is in me and God is here, there and all over."

THE GREATEST NEED

The greatest human need is love. The absence of love is the main cause of disharmony, maladjustment, failure, divorce, aggression and war.

LOVE

Where there is love, there is deep respect & trust
Where there is love, there is joy
Where there is joy, there is harmony
Where there is love, there is light
Where there is love, the future is bright
Where there is love, there is peace
Where there is peace, there is unity
Where there is unity, there is prosperity
Where there is love, there is no hate in society
Where there is love, thoughts have purity
Where there is love, each act creates beauty
Where there is love, there are no limits; love goes to infinity
Where there is love, the hearts feel serenity
Where there is love, there is calmness & charity
Where there is love, that is the highest prayer & sacred activity
Above all, where there is love, there is God & humanity

SELF-ESTEEM

Self-esteem is an experience of the inner self. Self-esteem does not come from color, race, religion, work, power or money. No one is perfect in this world. Each individual has strengths and weaknesses. Your self-esteem will always remain higher when you respect yourself, believe in yourself, behave well, and respect others and when you receive respect and support from others.

BEST GIFT

The whole world moves on the basis of the exchange of money, service and objects. The best gift is not a material object. The best gift is unconditional love which unites hearts. When there is a oneness of lover and beloved, love blossoms like a beautiful flower and remains alive forever. Love is something unique, and the more you give, the more you receive, so stop blaming and hating yourself and others for failures/problems/ maladjustments. Just open the fountain of love in your heart and merge deeply in love with your loved one. Share your love with others.

"Love is God and God is love. Love is the center of universe."

THREE MAJOR DEBTS

1. **Debt to God**: He who brought us to this world. This debt can be paid only through prayers, service to God and service to Mankind.

2. **Debt to Parents**: Those who gave us birth, love, care, attention, protection and education. This debt can be paid back only by giving back love, respect and help during old age.

3. **Debt to Teachers**: The teachers who gave us knowledge, support and guidance. This debt can be paid back through gratitude, money and gifts.

EGO, ANGER AND LOVE

All human beings are born with an ego. The ego plant grows in our mind as we watch our parents and society disliking others and discriminating against other social or racial groups. It also grows when parents say to their children, "You are the most handsome, beautiful, rich, superior and strongest person in your class, group or community and you should always be number one in your class, sports, music and other activities/ competitions." These statements and demands build the ego even stronger in our mind. Ego is like a little volcano and anger is the erupting lava. Anger starts with and escalates from external factors such as jealousy, hate, greed, impatience, frustration, competition, abuse, mistreatment and restrictive environment. Whenever you experience something negative in your environment or you feel angry, do not argue with the other person(s) as this fuels the fire. Simply listen quietly or walk away to a quiet area. Take three deep breaths and neutralize your anger with a contrary wave of love by using your soul consciousness and saying, "I will let this go. I will let this go. I will let this go." Then channel your energy into a constructive activity.

CHANGES OF LIFE

Change is the law of nature. We should not resist or react to change and we should not be afraid of the unknown as change might be good. One who resists or reacts to change without reflection is affected negatively. One who does not resist or react impulsively and accepts change adjusts faster and better and moves further with the changes and challenges in life. Remember that after every Sunset there is a Sunrise and after all suffering and pain there is pleasure.

PAST, PRESENT AND FUTURE

Everything moves in order in this universe. Nature moves effortlessly with real time where human beings move with psychological time making major efforts to obtain things. When any moment, day, month or year has passed, it becomes a memory and is history. When you live in the past and continue to carry bad memories and bad experiences to the present, then your present is affected. When you think of the future which is an illusion, again your present is affected and you loose a connection with your real self and real time. Thinking of the past brings sorrows and thinking of the future brings anxieties so learn to stay in the present moment by keeping 80% of your awareness and attention in the present, 10% in the past remembering what was good and what worked and 10% in the future to make sure that you are moving in the right direction. Use positive affirmations everyday, i.e., "I am in the present moment", "I am aware what I am thinking, speaking and doing", "I know where I am in my life and where I am going."

"The past is a history and future is a mystery.
Be wise and enjoy the gift of present."

HOPE

Nothing is permanent in this world. Life is a challenge and a struggle everyday, every month and every year. The strongest person is the one who faces the challenges, never giving up his/her hope for success and to meet God and continuing his/her efforts until he/she meets this goal. Hope is a beam of light in the darkness.

GREATEST PERSON

The greatest person is one who loves others and always sacrifices his time, efforts, money, possessions and life to help others without expectation of any reward. When the greatest person completes his mission of life and dies, then the whole world cries but he/she smiles.

GREATEST MASTER

God sends masters to give knowledge and guide the people on earth. A great master is never greedy and selfish. He/she is always humble. He/she loves everyone and educates others about God. The greatest master leads a very simple and spiritual life. He/she sacrifices his/her life for the sake of God, religion and people. Your greatest master will appear or meet you when you have detached yourself completely from material world and you are yearning to meet God.

SELF-REALIZATION

The world is a web of illusion. Human beings tend to become attached with their family, friends, possessions and places and they are always focused on fulfilling their physical and psychological needs (Physical needs are natural but psychological needs are unnatural and created by the mind). One who has great many possessions is far away from the real self and God. One who meditates and has few possessions is closer to the real self and contacts God. He/she finds real happiness and bliss within the self and not in the gratification of senses and nor in material things. His/her energy and attention move from lower level (body and ego) consciousness to higher level (spiritual and soul) consciousness. He/she unfolds the layers of illusion through his/her internal knowledge and attains the stage of self-realization (God consciousness).

SWEET SURRENDER

Sweet surrender means a total detachment from the material world and a total love, attention and devotion for God. No matter what you think, what you do or where you are, you have God consciousness with each breath. When you reach that stage, you will have no other desires except seeing God. You will feel total contentment when you drink the nectar of the name of God.

INVISIBLE COMPANION

When you have pure and unconditional love and a deep faith in God, he becomes your invisible companion. He blesses you, protects you in all difficult situations/problems, and guides you to the right path. Never feel lonely as loneliness leads to the lower consciousness. Always visualize God around you and remember that when God is near, there is no fear.

FOOD AND SELF (BODY, MIND & SOUL)

Food is the main source of energy and health. Without food, man cannot develop his anatomical body to the spiritual level. The sun radiates heat which evaporates water. The vapor becomes clouds from which rain falls to the earth. Man tills the earth and produces food which, when consumed, creates the energy that maintains the vigor. Vigor engenders discipline, which develops the faith that gives knowledge; knowledge bestows learning, which brings composure that creates calmness; calmness establishes equanimity, which develops memory that induces recognition; recognition brings judgment, which leads to the realization of "self".

"Eat natural and healthy food. Eat the food that does not cause excitement or laziness. Eat with patience and eat in silence. Always have positive thoughts, stay healthy and live longer happily."

INNER BALANCE

From childhood to adulthood, our attention is diverted from looking inward to looking outward and we start to see the world from outside looking in. Use your intelligence and willpower and change this pattern and belief about the world. Avoid doing things in excess as they disturb the mind and affect the inner balance. Go deep inside through silence, find a center and stabilize the center to recreate inner balance.

HEALTH

Health is the only real wealth. If health is lost, then happiness is lost. A body is healthy when the mind is healthy and the mind is healthy when there is a balance in the major areas/activities of life such as sleep, food, sex, relaxation, recreation, meditation, spirituality, discipline in character and routines, positive thinking, positive attitude, simplicity in life style and love and harmony in work and living environment.

Health means: H - Human
                         E - Energy
                         A - Awareness
                         L - Longevity
                         T - Tranquility
                         H – Healing

STRESS

Stress is a state of mind developed through our faulty belief system and an accumulation of negative thoughts, worries, unsatisfied needs, excessive work, fatigue and negative perception of the outer world.

"Beat stress by thinking positively and creatively, by organizing things, and making positive changes in lifestyle. Nourish relationship with others, eat healthy food, exercise, relax and meditate daily."

HEALING

The cause of mental and physical disease is deeply rooted in the subconsciousness. Visualize the cause of your problem by tracing your memories from present to the past. Do not get involved with emotions while you are tracing and reaching certain points. Keep moving further until you reach the root. As soon as you recognize the root, remove the root by forgiving the person(s) who hurt your emotions and use positive affirmations to seal that old emotional wound. Then healing will take place. You will be able to feel love, peace and joy and your consciousness will be clear like clean water.

VISUALIZATION

Visualization is an ancient method of meditation. Visualization is the simplest way to communicate with God and to see things of the past and future. You can recognize your inner child and you can heal your mind and body through visualization. The best method of visualization is to look at the picture of God, person or a flower for three minutes. Make sure that you do not blink your eyes. After three minutes, close your eyes and visualize the same picture or object for another three minutes in your third eye (located between the eyebrows). Increase the concentration of mind and the power of imagination through constant practice of visualization. Then you will develop a better reception system with the universe and you will be able to broadcast or relay better messages to others.

TWO SIDES OF THE HUMAN MIND

POSITIVE SIDE	NEGATIVE SIDE
Intelligence	Ego
Loveful	Possessiveness
Gentleness	Agressiveness
Natural	Conditional
Spiritual	Material
Godly	Brutal
Humility	Power
Receptive	Rational
Cooperativeness	Competitiveness
Contentment	Greediness
Creative	Destructive
Awareness	Ignorance
Helpful	Avoidance
Unselfish	Selfish
Feminine	Masculine
Humane	Animal Instincts
Introvert	Extrovert
Openness	Resistiveness
Freedom	Control
Practical	Careless
Kindness	Resentful
Patience	Impatience
Detached	Attached
Pure thoughts	Impure Thoughts
Intuitive	Impulsive
Active	Silent
Joyful	Sad
Peaceful	Rushness
Strong Willpower	Unknown Fears
Control Senses	Desires

PURIFICATION OF MIND

The mind is a driver and the body is a vehicle. The mind always controls and uses the body. The mind is the hardest thing to control. The mind always likes to possess where heart always likes to give. When the mind is cluttered with negative thoughts, emotions, greed, lust and desires, it loses concentration, creativity, inner peace and happiness. You clean your body everyday but you hardly have time to clean your subconscious mind. When old negative thoughts and resentments are stored for a long period of time in the mind, they become like stale food which stinks, becomes impure and causes indigestion and finally sickness. In the same way, old negative thoughts and resentments affect creativity, cause moodiness and block the flow of energy. They ultimately result in disharmony and disease. So clean your subconscious mind by writing negative thoughts on a piece of paper and then either shred the paper or throw it into the water. After this, purify your mind with prayers, have positive thoughts, write down your positive thoughts and goals and take good actions daily. Soon you will see magical changes in your life.

"Positive thinking is the key to knowledge, peace, joy, spiritual power and God"

MIND CONTROL

The mind is the single hardest thing to control. One who can control his/her mind, can control his/her life. The mind can be controlled if the following are learned and practiced in daily life.

* Meditation

* Deep Breathing

* Yoga/Exercise

* Relaxation

* Fasting

* Prayers

* Vegetarian/Non-Spicy Foods

* Living in a Peaceful Environment

* Positive Affirmations

* Positive Thinking

* Recitation of a Mantra

* Chanting

* Reading good books/Religious Scriptures

* Spirituality & Simplicity

* Practice to use willpower to control ego, anger, lust, greed and attachment

MEDITATION

Meditation is a process for uniting the senses and controlling the mind. Meditation is the only way to know the higher self and to connect the soul with the supersoul. Meditation increases universal awareness, soul consciousness, inner peace, concentration, calmness, creativity, intuition, memory, intellectual power and life span. Meditation decreases ego consciousness, anger, negative thoughts, negative energy, fears, mental/physical tension, heart rate, blood pressure, chemical imbalance, frequency of brain waves, impatience and hyperactivity.

Five Steps to Meditation

Peace - The environment should be peaceful
Place - The place should be clean
Position - Sit in a relaxed/cross-legged position
Power - Use willpower to control breathing and the senses
Purity - Have a pure heart and pure thoughts.

The best and simplest methods of meditation are as follows:

1. Practice to sit still in silence for 10-20 minutes daily. Even you cannot concentrate, simply sit and observe your own thoughts as these are the thoughts which have been disturbing you and keeping you away from the path of meditation. Try to recognize these thoughts and write them down on a paper and take appropriate actions to finish uncompleted tasks, unresolved personal/work/relationship problems and to make life more simple. Make a commitment to do meditation on a regular basis.

2. Place a small red light bulb or a red color paper in a oval shape or a God's picture on a white color wall in the range of your eyes and gaze on it for 3 minutes. Make sure that you

do not blink your eyes. Then visualize the red bulb, red oval shape or God's picture in your third eye (between the eyebrows) for as long as you wish.

3. Observe the tip of your nose for 3 minutes. Then bring your attention on the breath and slow it down from 15-20 times per minute to 5-6 times per minute. Then follow your breath like a shadow and feel the gap between two breaths.

4. When you breathe in, silently repeat the word 'SO' and when you breathe out, then repeat the word 'HUM' as many times and as long you can do so.

5. Use a bead necklace and recite God's name or a mantra 108 times. The most powerful mantra is Om.

6. Visualize your own spine and feel that white crystal energy is rising up from the base of your spine and moving up to your head and feel that blissful moment and the flow of energy in your body, mind and spirit.

7. Meditate on the sound of the river, ocean, waterfall or a soothing music.

NOTE: Perfection in meditation comes when you meditate at the same time and at the same place daily and attempt to reach the state of self-realization. When you reach to the final stage of meditation (samadhi) then there will be no other joy to experience. You will totally merge in God and you will have oneness with God. The best time to do meditation is before sunrise, before sunset and before going to sleep. If you feel scared to do any method or feel uncomfortable during meditation, immediately discontinue the meditation.

DEATH

What is born will die. This is the law of nature. Our body is mortal but the soul is immortal. Our birth and destiny of life is set by the Creator (God) based on the Karmas (actions) of our previous life. Before a soul enters into the womb, God gives certain amount of breath which we calculate into time (years). When we go through all stages of life (childhood, adulthood and old age) and spend all our breath, then life ends and the spark of soul leaves that body and enters into another womb. Some people die in an accident, violence, natural disaster or by committing suicide. Their death was written that way in their destiny before they came to this world.

We experience temporary death every second and every day when we exhale our breath, when we sleep or when we go into deep meditation. One Indian sikh Guru said, "Meditation is nothing but a rehearsal to die." In meditation, we obtain spiritual progress and practice to bring our soul at the third eye and connect it with supersoul (God) and soul's journey homeward begins. In the final stage of meditation (Samadhi), there is no desire, attachment, ego, fear, pain or suffering except blissful feeling and liberation and the holy spirit returns to God. Nothing material, family members or a friend goes with us when we die. The only thing that goes with us is our good karma. Always remember that life is short and death is definite, so do not struggle too much to achieve material success and then experience an ordinary and painful death. Increase God and death consciousness and practice the experience of dying simply and fearlessly through meditation while living. Then you will be able to leave this body at your will and you will not experience any pain and suffering when you die.

"Life is a journey from birth to death
The end of birth is death and the end of death is birth."

POSITIVE AFFIRMATIONS

Everyone goes through various negative experiences in life. Sometimes, we blame ourself and others for our misfortunes, losses, suffering, failures, etc. Blaming leads to low self-esteem and affects our mental and physical health and our daily relationships with people. Using positive affirmations can replace the negative thoughts and improves our overall perception of life.

Use positive affirmations when you relax. Besides the following affirmations, you may make up your own affirmations for any person or situation. You may speak each affirmation loudly so that you can hear them or you may repeat them silently.

1. I love my higher self.
2. I love my body the way it is.
3. I love my family.
4. I love my friends.
5. I love/respect all religions.
6. I love my country.
7. I love this universe.
8. I love God.
9. I love my work.
10. I believe in myself.
11. I am using my awareness to do things right.
12. I am changing myself and being more co-operative with others/things.
13. I am accepting all new changes in my life.
14. I am removing all negative thoughts/bad experiences from my mind.
15. I am controlling my anger/frustrations.
16. I am learning to cope with problems/situations of every day life.
17. I am removing old thoughts/beliefs/habits/resentment from my mind.
18. I am giving time to myself.

19. My health is more important than anything in this world.
20. I am being more disciplined in daily routines.
21. I am thinking more positively about everything.
22. I am making good decisions in my life.
23. I will do breathing exercises everyday as it unites my soul with the body.
24. I will meditate everyday.
25. I will not blame others for things/situations in my life.
26. I will not think hard about people/experience/future.
27. I will live more in the present moment.
28. I will not be afraid of people/things in my life. I feel strong about myself.
29. I am calm and relaxed everyday.
30. I will use my soul consciousness instead of ego consciousness in dealing with other people.
31. I will not be self-centered. I will help others in my daily life.
32. I am bringing more love, peace, and joy in my life.
33. I am open to communication with those whom I have never liked before.
34. I am going with the flow of life.
35. I am doing good things for my family, work, and society.
36. I am controlling my psychological needs.
37. I am controlling my impulses.
38. I believe in simple living and high thinking.
39. I will learn to heal my body with the power of my mind.
40. I am thinking better, feeling better, and doing better now.
41. I love nature which gives me real joy.
42. I am accepting all challenges in my life positively.
43. I am meeting the goals of my life.
44. I am learning to relax during all situations.
45. I will forget and forgive all those people who have given me a hard time in life.
46. I am improving my concentration and balance through breathing, meditation, laughter, and positive thinking.
47. I am being more humble/helpful/happy.
48. I am removing all anxieties/anger/doubts/hate/jealousy from my subconscious mind and I am filling it with love, truth, peace, patience, purity, and positive power.

49. I am getting to know more about myself everyday.
50. I am awakening my inner powers through meditation and by following all rules/laws of nature/God.
51. I am learning more about the reality of life. Nothing is permanent in this world and nobody is perfect. I will always be optimistic about good times and positive changes. I will focus constructively on my present.
52. I am taking myself from darkness to light by increasing inner awareness and controlling my negative thoughts.
53. I am following my worldly duties better now.
54. I am making positive changes in my routines and life style.
55. I am finding a center within myself by using breathing, yoga, meditation, and chanting methods.
56. I am being aware of my thoughts, emotions, instincts, desires and feelings and I am learning to control them in all the situations.

HUMAN AURA AND COLORS

Colors are the beautiful creation of God. Colors represent beauty, identify a person/objects and reflect desires, emotions, feelings, interests and the energy flow through human aura. The human aura contains different colors which move in a circle around the head and the chest area, just like some colors move around the sun and moon. You need to have higher consciousness, good observation power, psychic power and good intuition to read human auras. When you observe someone or you talk to a person, you will have flashes or psychic messages in your mind through your higher self about the colors, awareness, qualities, negative emotions and energy flow in the aura of that person. The spiritual person's aura contains white, yellow, orange and purple colors. These colors can be seen even two to five feet away from that person. The radiant colors are based on the person's emotional state. If the person is calm and relaxed, you will see blue and green colors. If the person is angry, you will see black color in the aura of that person. If someone has gone through lots of negative experiences, fear, stress, sickness or suffering, you would see grey and black colors in his/her aura and a weak flow of energy in the facial expressions, speech, body's chakras and the movements. The bad karma and bad experiences are stored and locked in the subconscious mind which affects the thoughts, emotions, mood, speech and actions. These suppressed emotions can be released only when the person confesses his/her sins, apologize to others, helps/serves God and others and make a commitment to lead a simple, natural and spiritual life.

You can use certain colors to bring changes in your thoughts, emotions and environment. The following are some of the colors and their significance:

White - purity, peace, healing, clarity in thoughts/energy, wisdom, light, cleansing, power, courage, simplicity, creativity, harmony

119

Sky blue -   calm, relaxed
Dark blue - knowledge, expression, discipline
Pink -   love, softness, beauty, good desires
Green - richness,   happiness,   growth,   harmony,   laughter, calmness
Red -   sex, strength, alertness, jealousy, tension, anger
Black - sex, death, stress, grief

Purple - spiritual awareness, psychic awareness, beauty, healing, stillness, gentleness
Orange -   simplicity,   sweetness,   purity,   pleasure, expressiveness
Violet - spiritual awareness, wisdom
Turquoise - coolness, pleasure, beauty, brightness
Yellow -   beauty, spiritual alertness, attention, intellect
Brown -   warmth, magnetic, internal force, greed
Tan -   simplicity, natural
Grey -   depression
Beige - intimacy
Gold -   power, radiant energy, richness
Silver - clarity
Lavender - spiritual knowledge, simplicity

18 DAILY RULES FOR SPIRITUAL PROGRESS

1. Wake up before sunrise and meditate.
2. Keep your body clean and wear simple clothes.
3. Eat fresh vegetarian food. Eat only when you are hungry and drink only when you are thirsty. Drink pure water and take in fresh air.
4. Feed birds, fish or animals.
5. Be helpful to others.
6. Be calm, cooperative, active and attentive during activities and interaction with others.
7. Discipline yourself and organize the things in your work/home.
8. Keep yourself occupied in constructive activities.
9. Maintain control over anger, lust and greed.
10. Maintain self-awareness and stay in the present moment.
11. Chant and read good scriptures during free time.
12. Don't criticize others and do not listen to the criticism of others.
13. Avoid indulgence and bad habit/bad company/bad activity.

14. Take a nap in the afternoon or relax to maintain balance in the body and mind.
15. Share love with others as love is God and God is love. When you give love, you give God to others and God will give more love, wisdom, help, goodness and beauty.
16. Acknowledge your responsibilities and keep your promises with others.
17. Keep purity in your heart and mind and cleanliness in your work and living environment.
18. Know thyself through meditation and devotion of God as knowledge comes through devotion and the personal experience of life.

THE PEARLS OF WISDOM FROM BHAGVAD GITA

1. Why do you worry so much? Why are you afraid of others? No one can kill you. The soul neither is born nor dies. What has happened that was good? What is happening that is good and what will happen that will be good also? You should not repent for your past, you should not worry about the future. Just focus on the present.

2. Why do you get angry or cry for your losses? You did not bring anything to this world, so you have not lost anything. What have you created which has been destroyed? Whatever you received, you received from this world and whatever you gave, you gave back to the world. You came into the world empty handed and when you will die you will go back empty handed.

3. Whatever you possess or own today belonged to someone in the past and will belong to someone in the future. What, you think, "I have great possessions and those are mine." You are happy because of these material things/possessions, but this happiness is the cause of your sorrows.

4. Change is the law of nature. What you think about death is not right, because death is actually life also. In one moment you become a millionaire and in another moment you become very poor. Remove all these words from your mind: my, mine, his/hers, ours/theirs, small and big. Only then everyone belongs to you and you belong to everyone.

5. Nothing in this universe is permanent. Everything is mortal. The only thing that is immortal is our soul. No one and nothing can kill this soul including men/women, weapons, air, water and fire. As you throw away your old clothes and acquire new clothes, so does the soul acquire a new body when you die.

6. You do not own this body and you do not belong to this

123

body. This body is made out of nature (earth, air, water, space and fire) and this body will dissolve into nature. What you are nothing but the soul is stable. Surrender yourself to God. He is the greatest helper in this world. One who knows about the help of God, always remains free from anxieties, fears and depression.

7. The senses are great, but greater than the senses is the mind. Greater than the mind is the intellect. Greater than the intellect is the spirit, the Supreme!

8. Constant striving for knowledge of the spirit, directing intuition for the purpose of knowing the truth, this is declared to be true knowledge (wisdom). All against this is ignorance.

9. When a man thinks of objects, attachment for them arises. From attachment, desire is born. From desire arises anger. From anger comes delusion. From delusion comes loss of memory. From loss of memory comes the destruction of discrimination, and from the destruction of discrimination he perishes.

10. Serenity of mind, gentleness, silence, self-restraint, purity of thoughts and feelings, this is called the tapas (austerity) of mind.

11. God is the light of all lights. Him they declare to be beyond darkness. He is wisdom, the goal of wisdom, to be reached by wisdom. He is seated in the heart of all.

INNER REFLECTIONS

- Our expressions (speech, movements and actions) are the reflections of inner self.

- The greatest healing power lies in love and faith in God.

- The true knowledge comes from devotion to God.

- You are not known by your beauty, power or wealth. You are known by your character, knowledge, good attitude and good deeds.

- The best philosophy of life is simple living and higher thinking.

- The highest duty of life is to help and serve others. Serving mankind selflessly means serving God.

- Love is not sex. Love is a powerful energy and gift of God which is only felt in the heart.

- Love is the source of all beautiful creations of this world. Unconditional love binds people and creates peace, joy and prosperity.

- If we want to change something in this world, we should change our negative thoughts, bad habits and negative attitude. When we change, the world changes.

- Do not dwell in the past what you have lost. Focus on what is left and where you are now in the present, where you have to go and what is the ultimate goal of life.

- Human life is full of changes, happiness, sadness and suffering. What we have within or what we receive from others, so we give to others. Always use humanistic approach.   Try to understand other's needs, concerns, problems, frustration, pain and discomfort. Show sympathy and compassion. Guide or help others. Love is something the more you give, the more you receive.

- Think creatively. Speak lovingly and act kindly. God has given us hands to help and heal others, not to hurt others.

- Intuition is a whisper of God to guide, help and protect those who have God consciousness. Share love with others and have good intentions to help others.

SPIRITUAL THOUGHT FOR THE DAY

Thoughts are the food of the Mind. Each thought interacts with each cell of the body. Whatever you think negative or positive, it affects the body in the same way. Subconscious mind is like a super computer. It stores every thought, impression, movement, action and experience. However, it has a limited capacity to store the information, especially the negative emotions, negative experiences and the resentments of the past. If you want to feed the new information, then you have to empty your subconscious mind, only then you can feed your conscious and subconscious mind with fresh and pure thoughts.

Life is very short. Each year, each day and each moment is very precious. Time is life and time is one brief micro-moment of an interlude of eternity. Enjoy each breath and moment everyday. Wasting time is wasting one's life. Start a new life now. Each day is God's day and each day is a new, beautiful and special day. Change your old perceptions, patterns and habits and start to see the days and world differently.

Monday -	Wisdom and actions
Tuesday -	Purity
Wednesday -	Hopeful, worryless, centeredness of being
Thursday -	Peaceful
Friday -	Loveful and joyful
Saturday -	Relaxation, meditation
Sunday -	Fun day, unity, charity, prayers, blissful and contentment

1. The first day of the month is the beginning of a new month and usually good begining has a good end. Do not worry what happened in the past month. Even you had failures but do not be discouraged. Maintain your self-confidence and enthusiasm to meet the goals this month. Put your mind and heart together into your work, do more constructive things, reform yourself and enjoy each day.

2. Every morning start your day with prayers and planning. Set goals for the day and take initiatives and actions to accomplish the goals. Even you cannot accomplish something by the end of the day. Do not worry and be patient as the world will not end tomorrow.

3. Everyone will try to become your friend when you have wealth and power but no one will come to help, when you are poor, helpless, or going through difficult time of life. A true friend is one who helps you in difficulties.

4. As the body is purified by the water, so is the mind purified by pure thoughts, prayers & meditation.

5. God is not only in church, temple or mosque. God is everywhere and among all human beings and dwells in the heart. The light of the lord shines in those who maintain a deep faith and who share love and knowledge with others. See God in each other.

6. If I have helped someone, I feel contented as my day has not been wasted.

7. Life has two sides like a river. One who stays in the middle is the safest, wisest and happiest person.

8. It does not matter how rich or strong a person you are but it matters how wise, humble, loving and caring person you are.

9. Real happiness is not in gratification of senses or in material objects. Real happiness is found within self.

10. Do not live in sorrow and do not give up your hopes. Hope is a beam of light in the darkness. A strong person is one who remains the same between joy and sorrows. Remember after every sunset there is a sunrise.

11. True knowledge does not come from the external world.

True knowledge comes when you detach yourself from the external world and turn your total attention inward and toward God.

12. When you love everyone, you have no enemy and when you have no enemy your thoughts, energy, time, actions and money is not being wasted and you live a peaceful life.

13. Everything is important but giving time to self, family and God are the most important principles of life.

14. Pearls are not found on the shores of the ocean, one has to dive deep into the ocean to find the pearls. The same way, money and success do not grow on trees. One who withdraws his/her energy and attention from several goals to one goal and uses wisdom, patience, interpersonal skills and work hard, he/she achieves success in life.

15. Today I am in the middle of the month. I will spend five minutes to think, look or review the things of the past two weeks, and I will spend five minutes to plan and prioritize my work for next two weeks. I know, I am doing better as God is with me and around me. When God is near there is no fear.

16. A smile creates happiness and makes others feel better and important, then why not I become a smile millionaire.

17. Do not do things excessively. Do things moderately. Balance is the key to happiness.

18. Gains and losses come and go but the wisdom of the wise and good deeds remains alive forever in the world.

19. One who is friendly, receptive, flexible and cooperative with others, he/she knows how to adjust with others and how to survive in difficult situations.

20. You do not need to boast or show others how wise you are. Your speech, actions and work are the reflection of your innerself.

21. Ego and anger are the causes of maladjustment, disharmony, destruction and suffering. When someone argues, swears or provokes, a wise man is one who does not react. He/she simply walks away, finds solutions to resolve problems and uses love, calmness and forgiveness to heal self and others.

22. Money is not the real wealth. Knowledge, gratitude and health are the real wealth. Ask yourself, "How wealthy am I?"

23. Worries make the mind weak. Find out the causes of your worries and remove the cause of your worries. When you control your needs and desires, your worries and sufferings are controlled.

24. It is easy to judge or blame others but it is hard to judge yourself. Always put yourself in the other person's shoes and realize how I would have done this thing or how would I feel, if I am questioned or treated this way?. Always treat others the way you want to be treated by others.

25. I do not need to express my love. The language of love can be heard by the deaf, it can be seen and felt by the blind and even animals.

26. If you want to know about the best person, then know thyself. When you know your real self, then you understand life and the world better.

27. The fact of life is that each action has a reaction. What you sow so shall you reap. So why not discipline self and love others. Love is something--the more you give, the more you receive.

28. Change is the law of nature. Do not be afraid of changes as changes might be good also. When things change, you should change and adjust with changes. Otherwise, you will be too behind and may suffer.

29. Accidents happen when you have conflicts, anger or lack of attention. Control your thoughts and use your awareness while doing things. No one can harm you and nothing can go wrong when you have God consciousness.

30 Do not follow everyone how they are doing things in their life. Keep yourself alert, active, curtious, disciplined and organized. Follow your own wisdom and insight and see what is right and good not only for yourself but for others also.

31. We all know where to apply commas and full stop. Then why not learn and practice to apply full stop on our negative thoughts, emotions, past negative experiences and move into a new month/year with wisdom, love, peace, joy, patience, calmness, happiness, unity, purity, stability, humility, simplicity and serenity.

PAST IS PAST.

BIBLIOGRAPHY

- Bhagvad Gita

- Mahanarayanopanisad

- Brihadaranyaka Upanishad IV 4.5

- Thoughts for Today - Raja Yoga Center, Mount ABU, India

- Mind Letters - J. P. Vaswani

- Hinduism Today

NOTES

GOALS

About the Author

Raj Kumar has written this book based on his real experience of two cultures East and West. He has gained spiritual knowledge through his parents, spiritual masters and practicing ancient methods of pranayama and meditation.

"Dr. Kumar speaks humbly and sincerely with words to encourage and inspire"
--Clifford Okumoto, M.D.
Psychiatrist

"This collection will make you stop and reflect upon what is really important in this life."
--Mark Dichner, Ph.D.

"This book will tap your inner wisdom to discover divine within!"
--Vasanthi Bhat, Author

The Power of Conscious Breathing in Hatha Yoga